AF372180

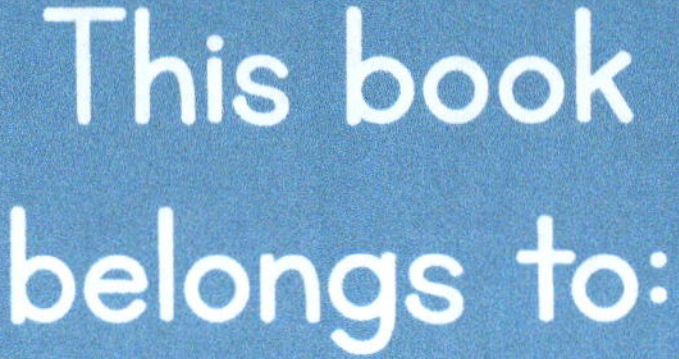
This book
belongs to:

Copyright© 2023. All rights reserved.

No part of this publication may be reproduced, distributed, or transmitted in any form or by any means, including photocopying, recording, or other electronic or mechanical methods, without the prior written permission of the publisher, except in the case of brief quotations embodied in critical reviews and certain other non-commercial uses permitted by copyright law.

First published 2023 with an exclusive licence from the author to CHEETAH® Purrrrrrr Publishing, an imprint of CHEETAH® Toys & More, LLC (CHEETAH®).

Contact us: 1-860-781-1276, 1-876-909-6311 (WhatsApp),
info@mycheetahacademy.com; paulettetrowers@yahoo.com

ISBN-13: 979-8-3303-4933-3
ISBN-10: 8-3303-4933-3

Dear CHEETAH® family:

Our little books were specially created to help our early readers master their decoding skills and build reading fluency. The repetitive use of high-frequency words, word families, decodable words, rhymes, and vivid illustrations facilitates this process. Our stories complement the objectives and content highlighted in the Jamaica Early Childhood Curriculum Guide and the Ministry of Education and Youth Grade I National Standards Curriculum.

In journeying through our series, our little ones will develop a deeper awareness of, and appreciation for, our Jamaican culture. Our books also have universal appeal, as any early reader can identify with the characters, events and subjects in our texts. Readers will get to enjoy the stories, build vocabulary, and exercise critical thinking by engaging in the activities at the end of each story.

Additionally, as a precursor to our series, or as a support to it, we've created a

decodable 'sentence strip' book for the very young readers and those who require more scaffolding.
Happy reading!

CHEETAH®

Chasing and capturing your dreams with you.

Letters are like the building blocks of a grand castle made of stories. Let's go! Let's build castles with words!

My decodable words:

bad, Dad, had, bed, shed, Ted,
pet, vet, did, lid, dip, ship, duck,
luck, fun, sun, not, pot

Letter sounds:

- consonant sound /d/ in the initial and final positions in words

- consonant digraph sound /sh/ in the initial and final positions in words.

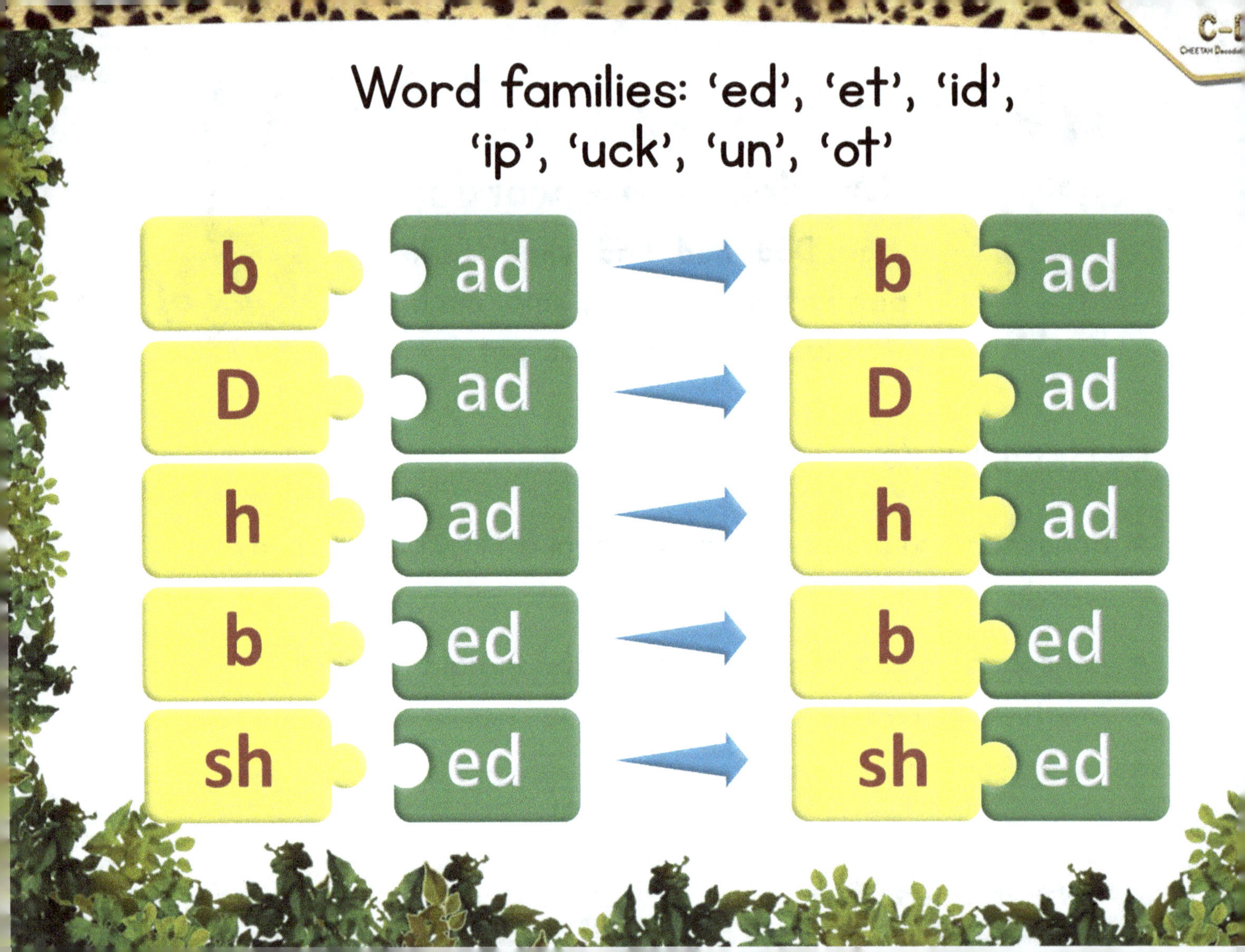

Word families: 'ed', 'et', 'id', 'ip', 'uck', 'un', 'ot'
b ad
D ad
h ad
b ed
sh ed
b ad
D ad
h ad
b ed
sh ed

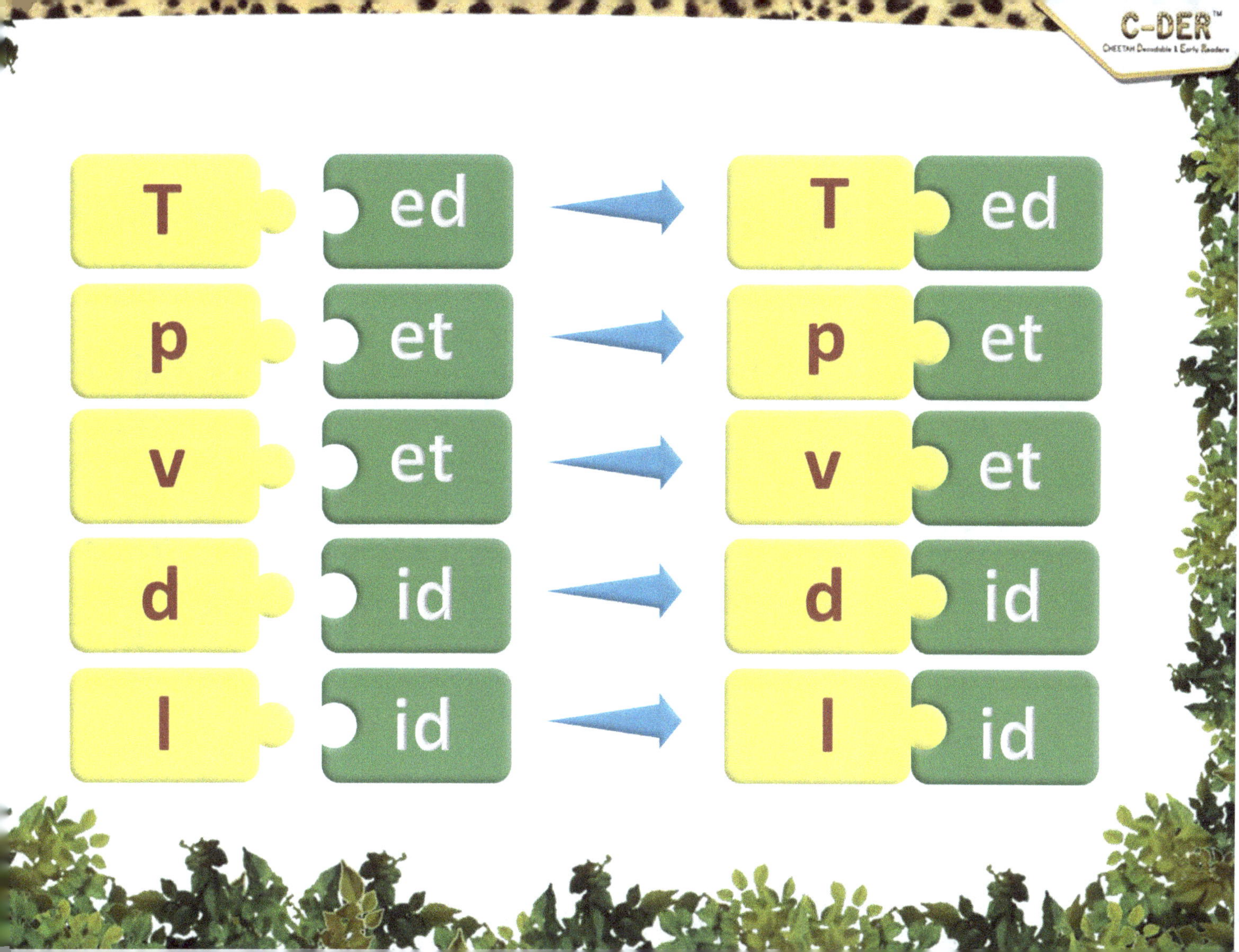
T ed
p et
v et
d id
l id
T ed
p et
v et
d id
l id

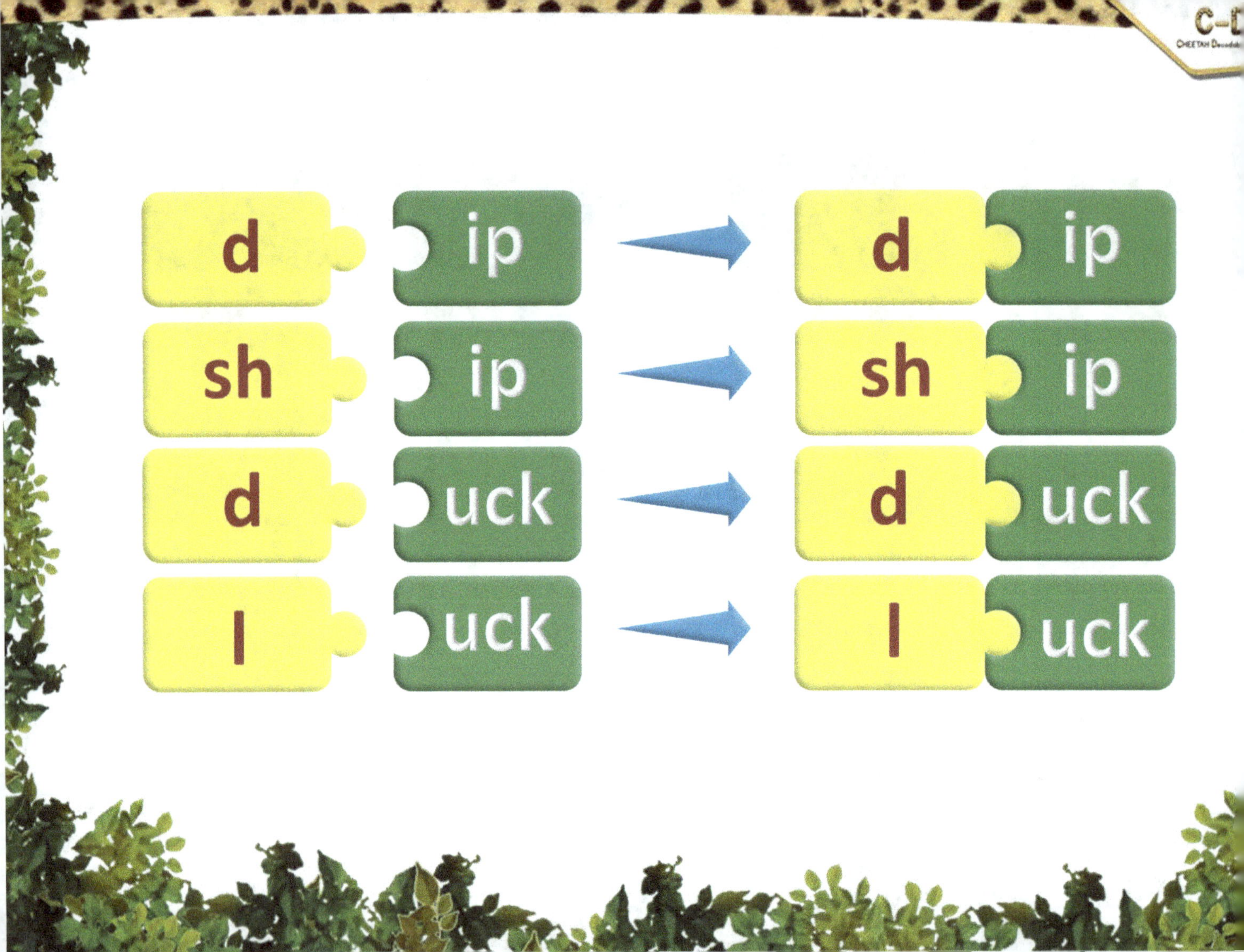

d ip
sh ip
d uck
l uck
d ip
sh ip
d uck
l uck

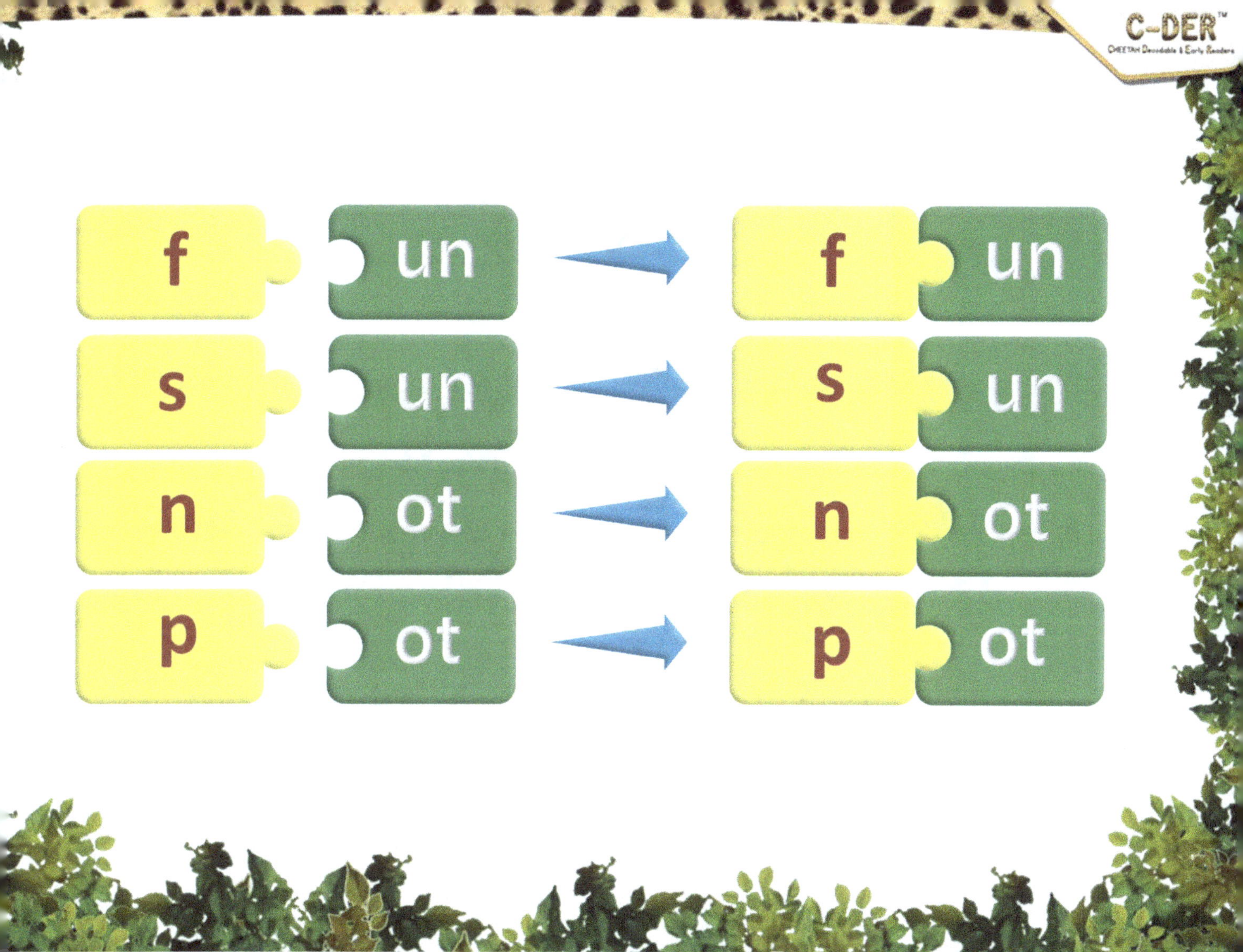

f
un
s
un
n
ot
p
ot
f un
s un
n ot
p ot
C-DER

C-DER
CHEETAH Decodable & Early Readers
1

'Dad, I wish I were a fish,' says Ted.
'I will never have to make my bed.
Each day, in the water, I will dip,
and I will swim along with every ship.'

3

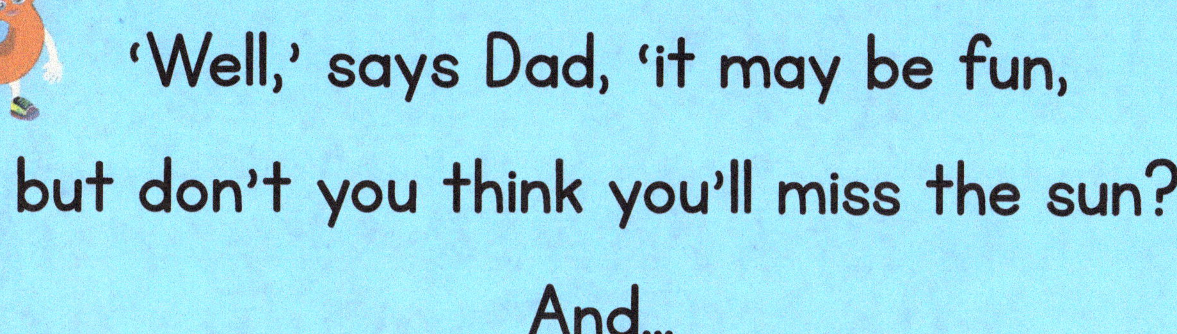

'Well,' says Dad, 'it may be fun,

but don't you think you'll miss the sun?

And...

What if someone has a wish for fish?

Then you will end up in a dish!'

'Hmmmm...' says Ted... 'Well, I have a new wish.

I do not wish to be a fish.

I wish I were a duck instead,

then I will have both the water and sun,' says Ted.

'Mrs. Dee had a duck; do you know what she did?

She put him to cook in a pot with a lid.

He was lunch that day; it was very nice:

duck meat cooked with peas and rice.'

Ted says, 'Well, ducks seem to have bad luck,

so I do not wish to be a duck.

I want to be a dog,' says Ted.

'Yes, I wish to be a dog instead.'

'Well,' says Dad, 'A dog is a good pet, and you have always liked the vet. You do not have to make your bed. You will sleep in the yard or in the shed.'

'We will have to give away your toys
to other little girls and boys.

'You know what, Dad?' Ted shakes his head.

'I think I will just make my bed.'

15

'I do not wish to be a fish
to end up one day on a dish.
A duck or dog I will never be,
because I am happy being me!'

Discussion and activities:

1. Have the children talk about the chores they do at home. Have them say which ones they like to do and don't like to do.

2. Have the children identify the words with the target letters and sounds.

3. Have the children make the sounds of the target letters and identify rhyming words in the text.

Discussion and activities:

4. Discuss the words: dip and lid as used in the context of the story.

5. Have the children read the text aloud.

Questions:

1. Do you love being yourself? What do you love most about yourself?

....

2. At what time of day you think the story is taking place? Why do you think so?

....

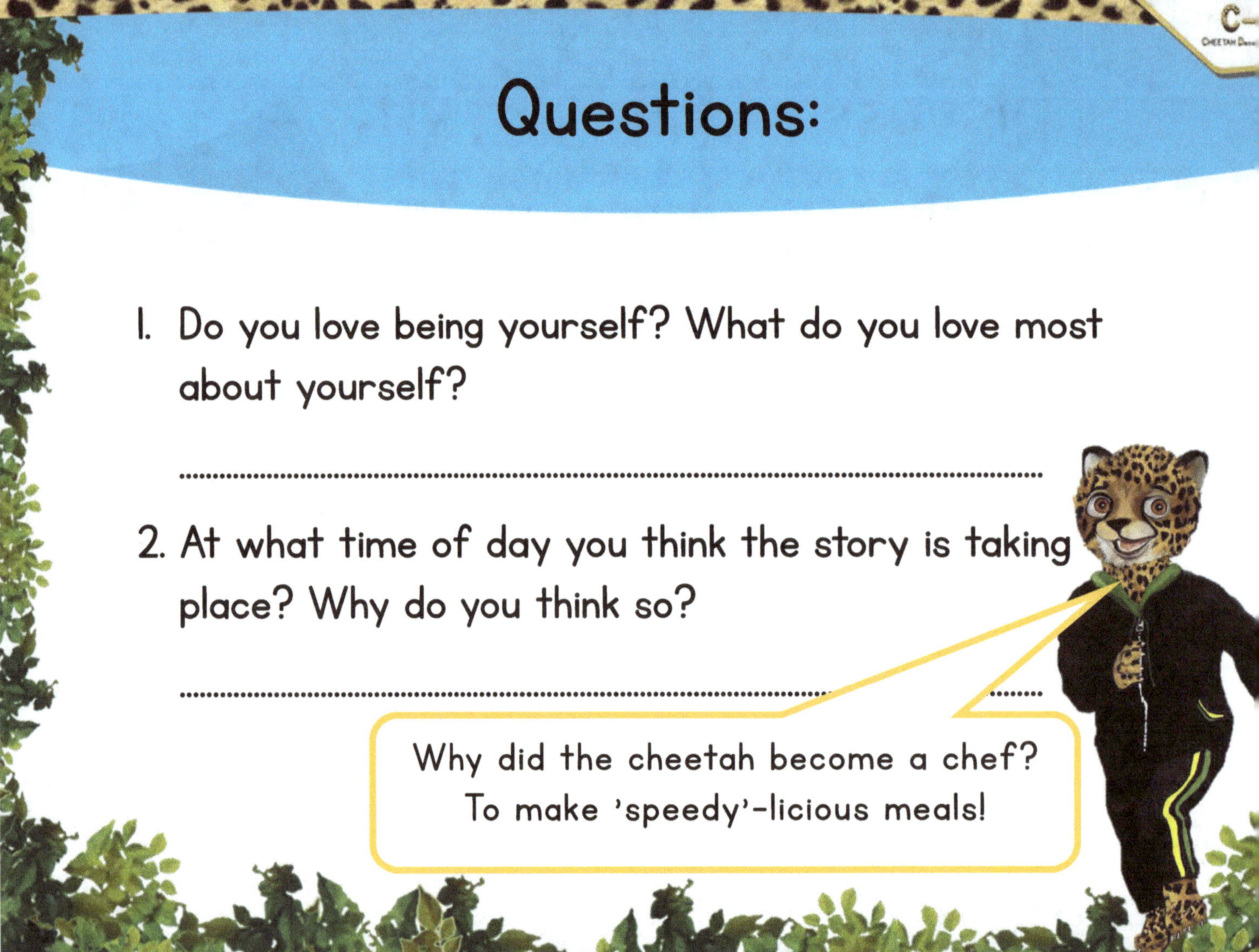

www.ingramcontent.com/pod-product-compliance
Lightning Source LLC
Chambersburg PA
CBHW081305130726
47998CB00010B/2934